HOW OLD?!

Quips and Quotes for Growing Older, Not Wiser

summersdale

HOW OLD?!

An Hachette UK Company
www.hachette.co.uk

Summersdale Publishers Ltd
Part of Octopus Publishing Group Limited
Carmelite House
50 Victoria Embankment
LONDON
EC4Y 0DZ
UK

www.summersdale.com

Printed and bound in China

ISBN: 978-1-78685-494-0

Substantial discounts on bulk quantities of Summersdale books are available to corporations, professional associations and other organisations. For details contact general enquiries: telephone: +44 (0) 1243 771107 or email: enquiries@summersdale.com.

To.............................

From..........................

You're how old?!

Housework can't kill you, but why take a chance?

PHYLLIS DILLER

Age is just a number. It's totally irrelevant unless, of course, you happen to be a bottle of wine.

JOAN COLLINS

GOOD CHEEKBONES
ARE THE BRASSIERE
OF OLD AGE.

Barbara de Portago

Anyone can get old.
All you have to do is
live long enough.

GROUCHO MARX

One of the best parts
of growing older?
You can flirt all you
like since you've
become harmless.

LIZ SMITH

'I've just got to put my shoes on and then I'll be ready,' lied Henrietta.

Don't worry about avoiding temptation – as you grow older, it starts avoiding you.

ANONYMOUS

If you survive
long enough, you're
revered – rather like
an old building.

KATHARINE HEPBURN

I got my figure back after giving birth. Sad, I'd hoped to get somebody else's.

CAROLINE QUENTIN

YOU KNOW YOU'RE GETTING OLD WHEN A FOUR-LETTER WORD FOR SOMETHING PLEASURABLE TWO PEOPLE CAN DO IN BED TOGETHER IS R-E-A-D.

Denis Norden

I have everything I had 20 years ago, only it's all a little bit lower.

GYPSY ROSE LEE

'Oh great, it's time for the housework,' said no woman ever.

A true friend remembers your birthday but not your age.

ANONYMOUS

Life was a funny thing that happened to me on the way to the grave.

QUENTIN CRISP

IF I HAD MY LIFE TO LIVE OVER AGAIN, I'D MAKE THE SAME MISTAKES, ONLY SOONER.

Tallulah Bankhead

It's sex, not youth,
that's wasted on
the young.

JANET HARRIS

Minds ripen at
very different ages.

ELIZABETH MONTAGU

'Of course the dye job looks natural,' Alice's friends said gamely.

The way I see it, you should live every day like it's your birthday.

PARIS HILTON

As you get older, the pickings get slimmer, but the people don't.

CARRIE FISHER

Time and trouble will tame an advanced young woman, but an advanced old woman is uncontrollable by any earthly force.

DOROTHY L. SAYERS

THERE'S ONE
ADVANTAGE
TO BEING 102.
NO PEER PRESSURE.

Dennis Wolfberg

To stop ageing – keep on raging.

MICHAEL FORBES

Past a certain point, no amount of fruit and veg can stop the ageing process.

Age is not different from earlier life as long as you're sitting down.

MALCOLM COWLEY

Middle age is when you are not inclined to exercise anything but caution.

ARTHUR MURRAY

TIME IS A DRESSMAKER SPECIALISING IN ALTERATIONS.

Faith Baldwin

Our ability to delude ourselves may be an important survival tool.

JANE WAGNER

Middle age is when you're sitting at home on a Saturday night and the telephone rings and you hope it isn't for you.

OGDEN NASH

'How could the shop be sold out of Prosecco?'

The best way to get a husband to do anything is to suggest that he is too old to do it.

FELICITY PARKER

Wrinkles are hereditary. Parents get them from their children.

DORIS DAY

I'm like old wine. They don't bring me out very often, but I'm well preserved.

ROSE FITZGERALD KENNEDY

AGE IS A HIGH PRICE TO PAY FOR MATURITY.

Tom Stoppard

Old age is an excellent time for outrage. My goal is to say or do at least one outrageous thing every week.

MAGGIE KUHN

Of course the side effect of eating so many greens to improve her cholesterol was that Edith suffered a chronic case of wind.

Old age is no place
for sissies.

BETTE DAVIS

Life is a moderately good play with a badly written third act.

TRUMAN CAPOTE

IT'S TRUE, SOME WINES IMPROVE WITH AGE. BUT ONLY IF THE GRAPES WERE GOOD IN THE FIRST PLACE.

Abigail Van Buren

Whatever you may look like, marry a man your own age – as your beauty fades, so will his eyesight.

PHYLLIS DILLER

There is no need to do any housework at all. After the first four years the dirt doesn't get any worse.

QUENTIN CRISP

'Hettie, I have to tell you, your hearing aid is broken. Now about those "silent" farts after dinner...'

Why is birthday cake the only food that you can blow on and spit on and everybody rushes to grab a piece?

BOBBY KELTON

If I'm feeling really wild, I don't floss before bedtime.

JUDITH VIORST

Nothing is more responsible for the good old days than a bad memory.

FRANKLIN PIERCE ADAMS

YOU CAN'T TURN
BACK THE CLOCK.
BUT YOU CAN WIND
IT UP AGAIN.

Bonnie Prudden

A woman is as old as she looks before breakfast.

EDGAR WATSON HOWE

Mary and Wanda strenuously denied signing up to the gym to see the handsome young personal trainer.

The elderly don't drive that badly; they're just the only ones with time to do the speed limit.

JASON LOVE

Like many women my age, I am 28 years old.

MARY SCHMICH

I'M AS OLD AS
MY TONGUE AND
A LITTLE BIT OLDER
THAN MY TEETH.

Anonymous

Seize the moment. Remember all those women on the *Titanic* who waved off the dessert cart.

ERMA BOMBECK

Remember that the most valuable antiques are dear old friends.

H. JACKSON BROWN JR

Double cream was much cheaper than face cream and probably did as much good.

When you are about
35 years old, something
terrible always
happens to music.

STEVE RACE

The easiest way to diminish the appearance of wrinkles is to keep your glasses off when you look in the mirror.

JOAN RIVERS

Please don't retouch my wrinkles. It took me so long to earn them.

ANNA MAGNANI

AS FOR ME, EXCEPT FOR AN OCCASIONAL HEART ATTACK, I FEEL AS YOUNG AS I EVER DID.

Robert Benchley

Beautiful young people
are accidents of nature,
but beautiful old people
are works of art.

ELEANOR ROOSEVELT

Finally, she had found a wine glass big enough.

Each year it grows harder to make ends meet – the ends I refer to are hands and feet.

RICHARD ARMOUR

I was born in 1962. True. And the room next to me was 1963.

JOAN RIVERS

I DON'T WANT A FLU JAB. I LIKE GETTING FLU. IT GIVES ME SOMETHING ELSE TO COMPLAIN ABOUT.

David Letterman

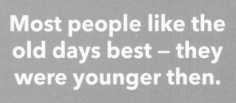

Most people like the old days best — they were younger then.

ANONYMOUS

I have bursts of
being a lady, but it
doesn't last long.

SHELLEY WINTERS

'Now, is this a hot flush or a particularly warming cup of tea?'

**Exercise daily.
Eat wisely. Die anyway.**

ANONYMOUS

An archaeologist is the best husband a woman can have. The older she gets the more interested he is in her.

AGATHA CHRISTIE

A woman never forgets her age – once she decides what it is.

STANLEY DAVIS

THE SECRET OF STAYING YOUNG IS TO LIVE HONESTLY, EAT SLOWLY AND TO LIE ABOUT YOUR AGE.

Lucille Ball

I don't plan to grow old gracefully; I plan to have facelifts until my ears meet.

RITA RUDNER

If she'd have known getting a hearing aid meant she had to listen to people again, she wouldn't have bothered.

The age of a woman doesn't mean a thing. The best tunes are played on the oldest fiddles.

RALPH WALDO EMERSON

Inside every older person is a younger person wondering what the hell happened.

CORA HARVEY ARMSTRONG

YOUTH WOULD BE
AN IDEAL STATE IF
IT CAME A LITTLE
LATER IN LIFE.

H. H. Asquith

I do wish I could tell you my age but it's impossible. It keeps changing all the time.

GREER GARSON

Don't let ageing
get you down. It's too
hard to get back up.

JOHN WAGNER

If Wilma never got another ruddy puzzle for her birthday it would be too soon. And you could stuff your sudoku too.

We are always the
same age inside.

GERTRUDE STEIN

I'd like to grow
very old as slowly
as possible.

IRENE MAYER SELZNICK

I plan on growing old much later in life, or maybe not at all.

PATTY CAREY

I AM GETTING TO AN AGE WHEN I CAN ONLY ENJOY THE LAST SPORT LEFT. IT IS CALLED HUNTING FOR YOUR SPECTACLES.

Edward Grey

The older one
grows, the more one
likes indecency.

VIRGINIA WOOLF

'Well I've proved I can still get my leg up there,' mused Dotty, 'But how in the Dickens do I get it down again?'

You know you're getting old when the candles cost more than the cake.

BOB HOPE

Old age at least gives me an excuse for not being very good at things.

THOMAS SOWELL

I BELIEVE IN LOYALTY; I THINK WHEN A WOMAN REACHES AN AGE SHE LIKES SHE SHOULD STICK TO IT.

Eva Gabor

It is sad to grow old
but nice to ripen.

BRIGITTE BARDOT

To win back my youth...
there is nothing I wouldn't
do – except take exercise,
get up early, or be a useful
member of the community.

OSCAR WILDE

Agatha tried not to let her disappointment show when her friend misheard and bought her a nice big clock for her birthday.

If they don't have chocolate in heaven, I'm not going.

ROSEANNE BARR

If you're interested in finding out more about our books, find us on Facebook at **Summersdale Publishers** and follow us on Twitter at **@Summersdale**.

www.summersdale.com

IMAGE CREDITS

Photographs © Everett Collection/Shutterstock.com

pp.3, 9, 16, 25, 32, 41, 48, 57, 64, 73, 80, 89, 96, 105, 112, 121 © Shelby Allison/Shutterstock.com